LONDON

AND ITS MOST

GROSS

DISGUSTING

AMAZING

YUCKY

SICK

FACTS

EVER!

HOMETOWN WORLD

How well do you know London?

You probably know quite a lot if you live here. Everyone knows that the Queen lives in Buckingham Palace, that Nelson's Column is in Trafalgar Square and that Big Ben strikes on the hour and chimes every quarter of an hour.

But did you know that, in 1858, London suffered from the Great Stink? Or can you guess how many bodies the River Police rescue from the Thames every year? How about the name of the man who fell into his toilet and drowned?

No? Well read on. You are about to find out some less well-known facts about London that might make your flesh creep and your hair stand on end…

Written by Jim Pipe
Illustrated by Tim Hutchinson, Leighton Noyes,
Nick Shewring and Tim Sutcliffe
Designed by Sarah Allen

First published by Hometown World Ltd in 2012
Hometown World Ltd
7 Northumberland Buildings
Bath BA1 2JB
www.hometownworld.co.uk

Copyright © Hometown World Ltd 2012

ISBN: 978-1-84993-250-9

CONTENTS

Poohy Poor

WANTED

Orange Boy
About 11 years old, this boy carries a basket of oranges for sale while pick-pocketing innocent young ladies.
5th March, 1850

Bridewell, once a palace belonging to Henry VIII, became a House of Correction. It provided meaningless work, such as the treadmill, for those receiving poor relief, to 'discourage them from idleness'.

What a life!
In 1901, a man could expect to live until he was 45 years old. Women were luckier – their life expectancy was 49 years!

Thames River Police recover more than 50 bodies from the river each year, some of which are unknown homeless people.

Right up until the 20th century, poor chaps who couldn't afford a divorce might raise some cash by selling their wives, even though it was illegal!

Poor Law, 1601

There were three kinds of poor folk.

IMPOTENT POOR: the old and infirm
ABLE-BODIED POOR: fit enough to work
PERSISTENT IDLER: lazy, idle, good-for-nothing scroungers who must be punished in a House of Correction!

Beggars Belief!

In 1531, a new law allowed the old and disabled poor to be given a licence to beg. Some people pretended to be mad or disabled in order to beg!

In Tudor times, poor people who were caught begging in the streets could be beaten all the way to the parish boundary.

EVIDENCE

Poor Londoners were often sent to prison if they owed money. In 1729, 300 people starved to death in just three months at Marshalsea prison, Southwark.

Gin

The poor may not have had much to eat in the 1700s but they had more than enough to drink. Gin was cheap and drinking became a big problem!

Revolting Rich Folk

In 1609, Sir George Wharton and Sir James Stewart fought a duel at Islington over a game of cards. Both men died.

In the 1800s, a stag chased by hunting hounds through Regent's Park ended up on the steps of 1 Montague Street, Russell Square!

What a waste!

The rich may have had a lot of money in the 1800s, but they knew how to lose it. Gambling and losing at the card tables was common!

WANTED

CHIEF EXECUTIVE

for large bank to earn squillions of pounds making tough decisions and telling people what to do. Rewards include massive bonuses.

18th October, 2008

In Tudor times, a nobleman would get 600 times more money than a labourer.

THE BANK

Pay

Date

£1,000

Do not mark below this line

Highwaymen were daring in the 1700s. Even George II was mugged in Kensington Gardens. He had his 'purse, watch and buckles' stolen.

VIP

1 5 1

Today almost 50% of Britain's millionaires live in London and the South East.

4 9 4 7

Servants

Really rich Victorian folk had servants to do all their work. Staff included a scullery maid, cook, parlour maid, housekeeper, lady's maid, butler, footman, stable lad, gardener and a nanny or governess!

In 1912, a hoard of 500 pieces of jewellery, hidden back in the 1600s, was found in Cheapside.

EVIDENCE George IV spent £24,000 on a cloak for his coronation in 1821. The cloak had a train 8 metres long. Even by today's standards that sounds a bit over the top!

Fancy an address at 1 Hyde Park? You'll need a cool £100 million for a penthouse!

Horrible Homes

The smallest house in London, 10 Hyde Park Place, measures just 1 metre wide.

On 20th October, 1660, Samuel Pepys wrote in his diary that his neighbour's cesspit filled up, flooding his own cellar with 'a great heap of turds'.

What a mess!

Until the 1600s, most cottages had a single room with an earth floor, open fire and a boxbed in the corner. Even animals shared the living space!

Poor Georgians often crowded into two-roomed homes where all the children crammed into one bed at night. When they all turned over, one often fell out!

In 1968, a corner of the 22-storey towerblock, Ronan Point in Newham, collapsed after a gas explosion because it was so badly built.

Home Comforts

Our idea of what's comfortable has changed over time. Here's a rough guide to centuries of new seating.

1500s: a hard wooden stool or bench
1700s: a woven-cane seat
1800s: a padded leather chair
1900s: a beanbag

Dodgy landlords bricked up windows to save money when a Window Tax became law in 1766, leaving tenants in the dark!

In Tudor times, half-timbered houses with thatched roofs were the fashion. Not a good combination with open fires and hot chimneys!

EVIDENCE

In the 1800s, row upon row of identical houses were built back-to-back for factory workers.

9

Foul Food

JELLIED EELS!
First, catch your eels in the Thames. Next, boil them with herbs. Finally, cool them to set in their own jelly.

What a feast!

Try a Tudor roast – a woodcock inside a pigeon inside a partridge inside a pheasant inside a chicken inside a guinea fowl inside a duck inside a goose inside a turkey! Feeling full yet?

Pupils at Westminster School have raced to catch a tossed pancake every Shrove Tuesday since 1753.

Poor Georgians often ate diseased and gone-off meat. The rich weren't safer, as rum, beer, wine and even tea contained poisons!

The Shambles was the name for an open-air meat market where butchers slaughtered animals, leaving the guts, offal and blood to run down a gutter in the middle of the street. Sausage, anyone?

Food Facts

People haven't always had the foods we enjoy now. Here's a rough guide to new foods over the centuries.

1600s: ice cream, sugar, potatoes
1700s: chocolate, tea, coffee, sandwiches
1800s: fish and chips, Heinz ketchup
1900s: sliced bread, fruit yoghurt

Until the modern refrigerator was invented in 1834, fresh food was difficult to keep.

People ate salted or smoked fish and meat, pickled fruit and vegetables, and dried beans and mushrooms.

In Cockney rhyming slang, 'pease pudding hot' means snot!

EVIDENCE

In the 1800s, poor children had such bad diets that they often developed rickets. This gave them weak bones and bowed legs and made their teeth fall out.

11

Chilling Childhood

Until 19.. teacher.. could punn.. naughty pupils with the cane, eitr.. across the han.. or the bottom.

The Spitalfields Nippers were street children who earned a few pennies chopping wood, cleaning window or running errands in the 1900s.

BABY FOR SALE

For as little as £10 or £12, poor Victorian parents sold their infants to 'baby-farmers'. Who knows what happened to the poor mites after that!

WANTED
Governess
for the teaching of french, embroidery, painting, music and dancing, in exchange for bed and board plus £20 a year.
31st March, 1841

What a crush!
Victorian teachers had to cope with up to 50 pupils in a class, often all different ages. Quiet at the back!

Help! My scho.. like a pris..

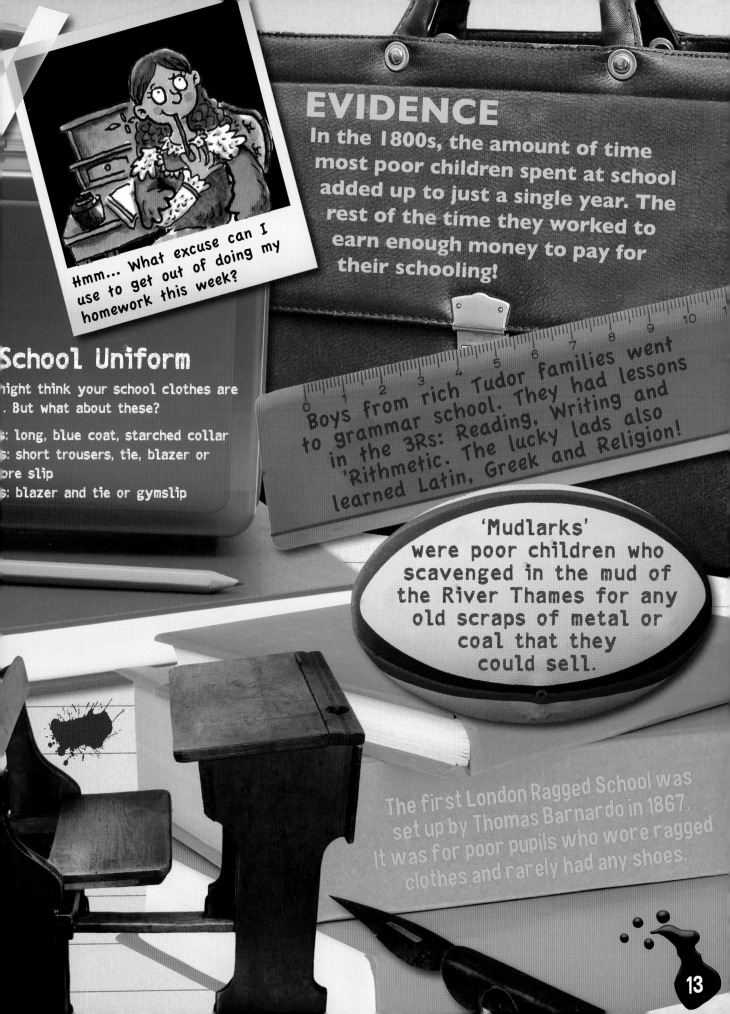

Hmm... What excuse can I use to get out of doing my homework this week?

EVIDENCE

In the 1800s, the amount of time most poor children spent at school added up to just a single year. The rest of the time they worked to earn enough money to pay for their schooling!

School Uniform

...might think your school clothes are ... But what about these?

...: long, blue coat, starched collar

...: short trousers, tie, blazer or ...re slip

...: blazer and tie or gymslip

Boys from rich Tudor families went to grammar school. They had lessons in the 3Rs: Reading, Writing and 'Rithmetic. The lucky lads also learned Latin, Greek and Religion!

'Mudlarks' were poor children who scavenged in the mud of the River Thames for any old scraps of metal or coal that they could sell.

The first London Ragged School was set up by Thomas Barnardo in 1867. It was for poor pupils who wore ragged clothes and rarely had any shoes.

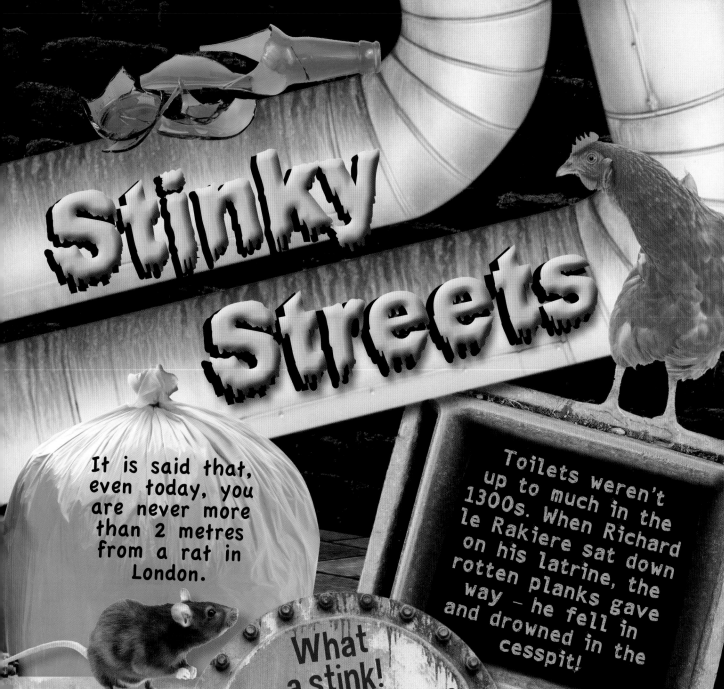

Stinky Streets

It is said that, even today, you are never more than 2 metres from a rat in London.

Toilets weren't up to much in the 1300s. When Richard le Rakiere sat down on his latrine, the rotten planks gave way – he fell in and drowned in the cesspit!

What a stink!

Until the Great Stink of 1858, people emptied their toilet waste into the River Thames – the same river they got their drinking water from! Excuse me, I'm feeling a bit queasy...

Instead of toilet paper, the Romans of Londinium used a sponge on a short wooden handle!

Henry VIII's courtiers at Hampton Court shared a mass toilet with 28 seats on two levels. The royal loos were cleaned by a team of 'gong scourers' – boys small enough to crawl along the drains!

Privy history

Happily, our toilet habits have changed over the years. Here's a rough guide to toilet accessories.

1550: chamber pot
1750: outdoor water closet
1850: outdoor flush toilet, newspaper
1950: indoor flush toilet, toilet paper

Even after sewers were built, our toilet troubles weren't over. Some sewers became so full that methane gas from the waste built up and exploded!

Can you guess what used to go on in Pudding Lane, Dunghill Lane and Threadneedle Street?

EVIDENCE

After umpteen cholera epidemics, the Grand Experiment began in London in 1845 to 1852. 300,000 people took part. Half drank water from the Thames (this was normal) and half drank clean drinking water. Guess what? More Thames water-drinkers died sooner!

15

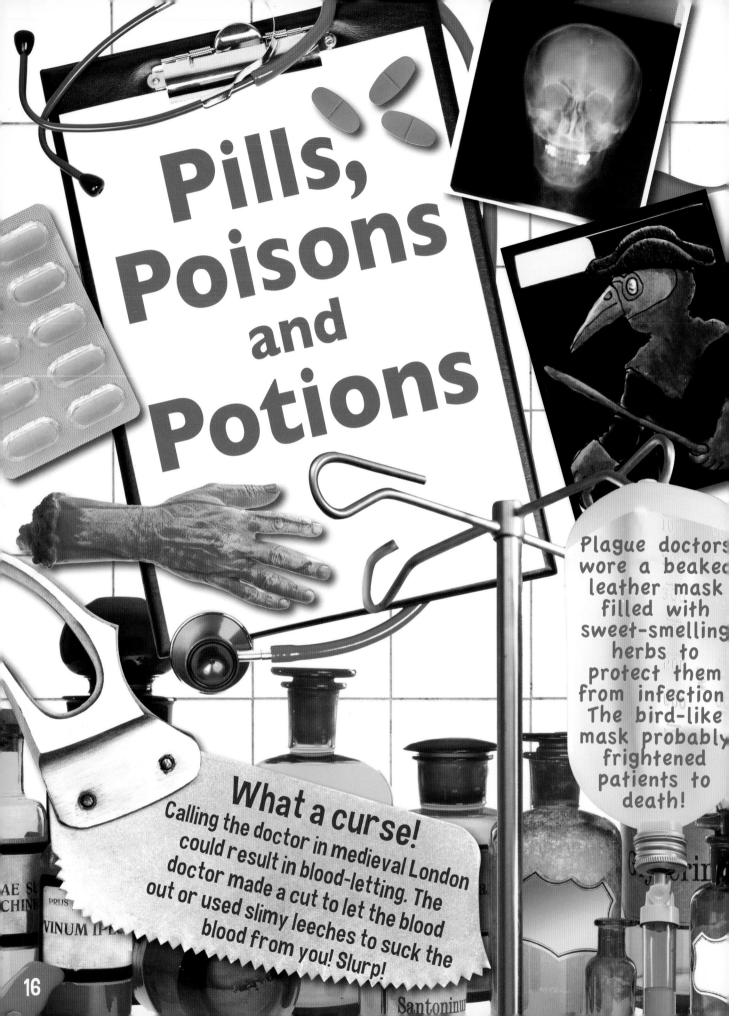

Pills, Poisons and Potions

Plague doctors wore a beaked leather mask filled with sweet-smelling herbs to protect them from infection. The bird-like mask probably frightened patients to death!

What a curse!
Calling the doctor in medieval London could result in blood-letting. The doctor made a cut to let the blood out or used slimy leeches to suck the blood from you! Slurp!

Dying for a cure

Medical problems have changed as cures have been found. Here's a rough guide to the biggest killers.

1600s: bubonic plague, sweating sickness
1700s: smallpox, typhus, scurvy, flu
1800s: cholera, measles, tuberculosis
1900s: flu, tuberculosis, polio

In 1403, patients at St Mary Bethlehem hospital could be chained up, whipped or poked. The hospital became known as Bedlam.

WANTED
Hospital mortuary attendant

To receive the deceased, assist in autopsies, arrange viewings for loved ones and organize disposal of unclaimed bodies and body parts.
17th July, 1889

Until the invention of anaesthetic in the mid-1800s, there was no pain-relief during surgery – unless you count biting on a piece of cloth!

John Gardner, a doctor from Shoreditch around 1800, removed worms from his patients, including one with '4 horns, 6 legs and 12 feet'!

Cures recommended by Georgian nursemaids included hare's brains for teething babies!

In medieval times, lepers at London's leprosy hospitals had to carry a bell to warn people to keep away.

EVIDENCE
The number of years you can expect to live has almost doubled since 1900, thanks to new medicines and better hospitals.

JOYLESS JOURNEYS

Colonel Pierpoint built the first traffic island to help him cross the road safely. In 1864, he tripped over it and was run over by a cab!

More than 4 million passengers take the London tube train each day.

ONE WAY

What a rush!
Wealthy Georgians in a hurry simply called for a sedan chair to be carried by two servants through the streets, whatever the weather. Come along, dear fellow!

WANTED
Claude Duval Highwayman for holding up coaches and demanding money and jewellery from passengers. Wears a mask. Dangerous – do not approach if found! 29th December, 1669

Thanks to an ancient law, London cabbies can't carry passengers who might have a 'notifiable disease', such as smallpox or bubonic plague.

London's first traffic lights in Parliament Square were run on gas. They exploded in 1869, injuring a policeman.

Elizabethan London was full of muddy ditches and potholes.

Getting about

Ways of travelling have changed over the years. Here's a rough guide to favourite forms of transport.

1600s: foot, horseback, stagecoach
1700s: sedan chair, canal boat
1800s: bicycle, train
1900s: motorbike, car, plane

End

The first London to Brighton car race in 1896 celebrated a new law that raised the speed limit from 4 mph (6 kph) to 14 mph (22 kph).

Push button wait for signal

WAIT

wait

cross with care

EVIDENCE
On 11 July, 2000, a London Underground driver fell asleep on the Northern line. The tube train rolled backwards for almost a kilometre with 100 people on board!

CRAZY CRIMINALS

WANTED

Guido Fawkes
A.K.A. Guy Fawkes, suspected of conspiring in gunpowder plot to blow up Parliament. 5th November. - 1605

The last hanging in Britain was on 13th August, 1964. However, capital punishment wasn't abolished until 1998.

The Kray Twins, notorious East End gang criminals, led a celebrity lifestyle before being jailed for murder in 1969. They both served life sentences.

What a waste! Over 70,000 people were executed during Henry VIII's reign!

Penalties

In Georgian times, criminals were given harsh punishments such as being whipped or dragged through the streets. In the 1800s, thousands were shipped to America and later Australia.

In Elizabethan times, the worst criminals were hanged, drawn and quartered. This meant that they were hanged by the neck until half-dead, then dragged behind a cart before being cut into four pieces!

EVIDENCE

Since 1987, DNA evidence has been used to identify criminals and to clear innocent people. DNA evidence can come from blood, saliva, hair or flakes of skin.

Witchcraft

In medieval times, ducking was a punishment often used for women suspected of being witches. The victim was strapped to a chair and plunged into water. Others suspected of witchcraft were burned at the stake.

Jack Sheppard, a pickpocket living in London in the 1700s, was arrested and escaped four times. Eventually his luck ran out and he was hanged at Tyburn.

THE DAILY NEW

9th November, 1888 · Your favourite local newspaper

C R A Z Y CRIMINALS, CRIMES AND PENALTIES

Jack the Ripper strikes again! The Whitechapel murderer is still at large. Police are baffled.

During the early hours of yesterday morning, another murder of a most revolting and fiendish kind took place in Spitalfields. This is the seventh which has occurred in this neighbourhood, and the character of the crime leaves very little

has com the pre o n e The scene this last cr is at No. Dorset Stre Spitalfield which is abou 200 yards distan from 35 Hanbury Street, where the unfortunate woman, Mary Ann Nicholls, was so foully m u r d e r e d . The latest victim's name is Mary Ann, or Mary Jane, Kelly. At about 1 o'clock y e s t e r d a y morning a person living in the court opposite to the room occupied by the woman heard her

WICKED WARS

BRITONS
Your Country Needs You!
To join Field Marshal Kitchener's army! Volunteer today to fight the war against the Hun. God Save the King! 5th September, 1914

Yeomen Warders, who are retired army officers, guard the Tower of London. They are nicknamed 'Beefeaters' because they may once have been paid partly with beef!

In AD 61, Queen Boudica led an uprising against the Romans and burned London to the ground. Around 70,000 Londoners were hanged, beheaded or crucified and their bodies thrown into the Thames.

What a war!
Parliament controlled London during the Civil War from 1642 to 1646, while the deposed king, Charles I, fled to Oxford.

Huge Zeppelin balloons dropped bombs on London in World War One.

The Victoria Cross is the highest military medal awarded for bravery in the face of the enemy.

SERIAL NO. CB 722595
(CHILD'S)
1954
RATION BOOK
Surname
Address

R.B.1
16
MINISTRY OF FOOD
1953-1954
SERIAL NO. 1
AU 684378

RATION BOOK

During World War Two, there were 2,000 London 'Restaurants' where families whose homes had been bombed could buy a meal for 9d (nine old pennies).

British Armed Forces

Britain hasn't always had an army, navy and air force. Read below to find out when they formed.

1500s: Royal Navy
1664: Royal Marines
1707: British Army
1918: Royal Air Force

EVIDENCE

Inside the Tomb of the Unknown Warrior, in Westminster Abbey, lies the body of an unidentified British soldier killed during World War One. He represents hundreds of thousands of soldiers who have died in battle.

In September 1940, London was bombed for 11 days, creating a firestorm during which 20,000 people died.

Ghastly Ghouls

Two sailors are said to haunt 50 Berkeley Square after coming to a sticky end there. One was found impaled on railings outside, while the other went mad. Mwaa-ha-ha!

Dick Whittington is buried in St Michael Paternoster Royal Church in the City of London. A mummified cat was found there in 1949 too. Meowooooo!

What a collection!
The Museum of London has over 2,500 skeletons of former Londoners.

WHITECHAPEL BODYSNATCHERS London surgeons who wanted to teach anatomy could buy a freshly dug-up corpse of a murderer for £4 in Victorian times.

During the Great Plague of 1665, 1,000 bodies were buried in a plague pit beneath where Aldgate Station is today.

In the 1970s, a vampire was said to have haunted Highgate Cemetery. A vampire hunt was held on Friday 13th March – unlucky for some!

EVIDENCE

Severe overcrowding in London's cemeteries led to the opening of the London Necropolis Railway in 1854. Funeral trains ran from Waterloo to Brookwood Cemetery, 50 kilometres away, carrying coffins and mourners.

Headless Ghosts

Executed prisoners are said to haunt the Tower of London. Could any of these unfortunate people be the guilty ghouls?

1483: Princes Edward V and Richard, Duke of York, rumoured to have been murdered

1536: Anne Boleyn executed

1618: Walter Raleigh executed

London's oldest burial ground on Parliament Hill dates from 2400 BC!

DEADLY DISASTERS

In 1987, a great storm toppled many of London's plane trees, blocking roads and crushing parked cars.

Friday, 11 June

Dialling 999 was the world's first emergency phone call service.

slide to unlock

What a wipeout!

When a huge vat of beer collapsed in Horseshoe Brewery in 1814, the wave of beer destroyed two homes and drowned eight people. What a way to go!

WANTED
Disaster Planner
to set up plans for managing natural and manmade disasters in the city. Must own a crystal ball!
1st January, 2012

An apprentice cobbler called Thomas Grey is the only known fatality of an earthquake in London. He was killed in Newgate Street.

No Smoking! Smoking was banned on the Underground after a discarded cigarette set fire to rubbish at King's Cross Station in 1987.

Eight people died in the Great Fire of 1666 yet most of the city was razed to the ground and 80,000 Londoners were left homeless. Lucky escape!

In December 2006, a tornado ripped through Kensal Green, injuring six people and damaging over 100 properties.

During World War One, 50 tonnes of explosives blew up at Silvertown munitions factory, killing 73 people and showering the area with hot metal.

EVIDENCE
The number of workers killed at work has dropped dramatically over recent years. Fatal injuries at work fell from over 600 in the 1970s to just over 100 by 2010.

Great Escapes

Here's a rough guide to rescue services throughout the centuries.

1730: First fire engine
1829: First professional police force
1829: First coastguard service
1914: First motorized ambulance

LOUSY LISTS

Top Ten Disasters

- [ ] 1348: Black Death
- [ ] 1665: The Great Plague
- [ ] 1666: Great Fire of London
- [ ] 1683: The Great Frost
- [ ] 1721: Smallpox
- [ ] 1832: Cholera epidemic
- [ ] 1858: The Great Stink
- [ ] 1918: Flu epidemic
- [ ] 1952: The Great Smog
- [ ] 1953: Great Flood
- [ ]
- [ ]
- [ ]
- [ ]

Rotten Workhouse Rules, 184

Any poor person who breaks these rules w
live on bread and water for 48 hours.

- Do not make a noise.
- Do not swear or use foul language.
- Do not insult another person.
- Do not threaten or hit another person.
- Do not refuse to wash.
- Do not refuse to work.
- Do not pretend to be sick.
- Do not play cards or gamble.
- Do not trespass in other areas of the workhouse.
- Do not misbehave at prayers.
- Do not get back late.
- Do not disobey an order from any officer of the workhouse.

Crazy Cures

- Carry a scrap of paper with the magic wo ABRACADABRA written on it.
- Drill a hole in the skull to let out the evil spiri
- A grey cat's skin can be used to cure whoopi cough.
- Cover a horseshoe with a red cloth to get rid of nightmares.
- Smoke tobacco to ward off the plague.
- Drink Holy water.
- Hang a dead toad around your neck as a lucky charm.
- Slice off boils and pustules.
- Bleed the patient either by cutting through a vein or putting leeches on parts of the body to suck out the blood.
- Consult a witch.

Peculiar Place Names

Amen Corner
Birdcage Walk
Bleeding Heart Yard
Change Alley
Crooked Usage
Coldbath Square
Fish Street Hill
Friday Street
Garlick Hill
Gunpowder Alley
Gutter Lane
Hanging Sword Alley
Houndsditch
Huggin Lane
Little Britain
Love Lane
Rotten Row
Seething Lane
Shorts Gardens
Turnagain Lane
Trump Street
Wrestlers Court

Wicked Witchcraft Rules, 1604

You must not use Witchcraft, Sorcery, Charm or Enchantment to:

1. find treasure
2. find lost or stolen things
3. make someone fall in love unlawfully
4. destroy property
5. hurt or destroy a person's body

Anyone found guilty will be imprisoned for a year, and once every three months will be put in the pillory for six hours on Market Day.

You must not use Witchcraft, Sorcery, Charm or Enchantment to:

1. conjure up any evil spirits
2. consult, employ, encourage or reward any evil spirits
3. take any dead bodies from the grave
4. remove the skin, bone or any other part of a dead body
5. kill, destroy, waste, consume or maim anyone

Anyone found guilty will suffer pain of death, and lose the privilege and benefit of Clergy and Sanctuary.

Bottom Ten Worst Ever Jobs

10. Job Title: Searcher of the dead (Medieval)
Job Description: Spot plague victims and mark their door with red cross.

9. Job Title: Tosher and grubber (Victorian)
Job Description: Scour London's sewers for anything of value.

8. Job Title: Flusherman (Victorian)
Job Description: Clear blockages in the sewer system.

7. Job Title: Match girl (Victorian)
Job Description: Work in a match factory with poisonous phosphorous, risking 'phossy jaw', a disease that rots your lower jaw.

6. Job Title: Rat catcher
Job Description: Trap as many rats as possible with the help of a trusty terrier.

5. Job Title: Fluffer
Job Description: Spend the night in the underground tunnels, removing human hair and dead skin which might be a fire hazard.

4. Job Title: Crossing-sweeper (Georgian)
Job Description: Sweep a path through mud and dung for rich ladies and gentlemen.

3. Job Title: Chimney sweep
Job Description: Climb up chimneys to brush out the black, dusty soot.

2. Job Title: Gravedigger
Job Description: Dig a hole 1.5 metres deep ready for burial. Then fill it in.

1. Job Title: Executioner
Job Description: Place a noose around the prisoner's neck, drop him from the gallows and allow to hang until he is dead.

QUICK QUIZ

1. When was the sandwich invented?
a. 1600s
b. 1700s
c. 1800s

2. What was the speed limit in 1896?
a. 12 kph
b. 22 kph
c. 32 kph

3. What was Bridewell?
a. House of Correction
b. House of Horror
c. House of Commons

4. Whose cellar was flooded by a 'great heap of turds'?
a. Samuel Beckett
b. Samuel Johnson
c. Samuel Pepys

5. How much did George IV spend on his cloak?
a. £240
b. £2,400
c. £24,000

6. Where is the Tomb of the Unknown Warrior?
a. Westminster Abbey
b. Westminster Bridge
c. Westminster Hall

7. How many people were executed during Henry VIII's reign?
a. 700
b. 7,000
c. 70,000

8. Who tried to blow up Parliament in 1605?
a. Jack the Ripper
b. Jack Sheppard
c. Guy Fawkes

9. What did the plague doctor wear to treat patients?
a. Rubber gloves
b. A leather face mask
c. A white sheet

10. Why were the Ragged Schools called that?
a. The head teacher was worn ragged by the children
b. The teachers wore second-hand gowns
c. The pupils wore rags

QUICK QUIZ ANSWERS

1. b. 1700s
2. b. 22 kph
3. a. House of Correction
4. c. Samuel Pepys
5. c. £24,000
6. a. Westminster Abbey
7. c. 70,000
8. c. Guy Fawkes
9. b. A leather face mask
10. c. The pupils wore rags

ACKNOWLEDGEMENTS

Cover: CG Textures; Andrew Buckin/Shutterstock; brokenarts/Shutterstock; Cherniga Maksym/Shutterstock; Colour/Shutterstock; Cosmin Manci/Shutterstock; Derek L Miller/Shutterstock; Kovalchuk Oleksandr/Shutterstock; glyn/Shutterstock; Kitch Bain/Shutterstock; Ligak/Shutterstock; Milos Luzanin/Shutterstock; Nick Barounis/Shutterstock; Pablo H Caridad/Shutterstock; Pakhnyushcha/Shutterstock; Pavzyuk Svitlana/Shutterstock; Philip Lange/Shutterstock; Robert English/Shutterstock; Ustyuzhanin Andrey/Shutterstock; val lawless/Shutterstock; hberends/Stock Exchange. p1: val lawless/Shutterstock. pp2/3: CG Textures; Adolfo Rodriguez Aguilar/Shutterstock; Andrew Buckin/Shutterstock; Angela Jones/Shutterstock; chrisbrignell/Shutterstock; fotoret/Shutterstock; homydesign/Shutterstock; Pakhnyushcha/Shutterstock. pp 4/5: CG Textures; Amy Johansson/Shutterstock; Barbro Bergfeldt/Shutterstock; chrisbrignell/Shutterstock; Kachalkina Veronika/Shutterstock; LockStockBob/Shutterstock; Olga Kovalenko/Shutterstock; Pablo H Caridad/Shutterstock; s.juchim/Shutterstock; SeDmi/Shutterstock; Steshkin Yevgeniy/Shutterstock; Valery Kraynov/Shutterstock; brokenarts/Stock Exchange; mordoc/Stock Exchange. pp6/7: Gregor Kervina/Dreamstime; argus/Shutterstock; Bragin Alexey/Shutterstock; Cherniga Maksym/Shutterstock; Christos Georghiou/Shutterstock; deskcube/Shutterstock; fotoret/Shutterstock; glyn/Shutterstock; LittleRambo/Shutterstock; Miramiska/Shutterstock; nadi555/Shutterstock; Pixelbliss/Shutterstock; schankz/Shutterstock; Scott Latham/Shutterstock; vladm/Shutterstock. pp8/9: CG Textures; Dja65/Shutterstock; H. Brauer/Shutterstock; Cosmin Manci/Shutterstock; Andrew Buckin/Shutterstock. pp10/11: SarahAllenStock; Allocricetulus/Shutterstock; Aprilphoto/Shutterstock; artkamalov/Shutterstock; Colour/Shutterstock; F.C.G./Shutterstock; guigaamarti ns/Shutterstock; Joe Belanger/Shutterstock; Kovalchuk Lizard/Shutterstock; Oleksandr/Shutterstock; OtnaYdur/Shutterstock; Pavzyuk Svitlana/Shutterstock; Petr Salinger/Shutterstock; spillikin/Shutterstock; Strakovskaya/Shutterstock; Tanis Saucier/Shutterstock. pp12/13: aelove7/Shutterstock; Africa Studio/Shutterstock; Borodaev/Shutterstock; FuzzBones/Shutterstock; Garry L./Shutterstock; June Scheffel/Shutterstock; karen roach/Shutterstock; negative/Shutterstock; Paul Cowan/Shutterstock; PRIMA/Shutterstock; Robbi/Shutterstock; Venus Angel/Shutterstock. pp14/15: CG Textures; Chutima Tunarang/Shutterstock; hsagencia/Shutterstock; kzww /Shutterstock; marema/Shutterstock; Marilyn Volan/Shutterstock; Vasyl Helevachuk/Shutterstock; Pakhnyushcha /Shutterstock; S.Dashkevych/Shutterstock; s_oleg /Shutterstock; Ustyuzhanin Andrey Anatolyevitch /Shutterstock; Vladimir Caplinskij/Shutterstock; pp16/17: CG Textures; Colour/Shutterstock; Foto Bouten/Shutterstock; Fribus Ekaterina/Shutterstock; Graeme Dawes/Shutterstock; gualtiero boffi/Shutterstock; Henk Vrieselaar/Shutterstock; Kitch Bain/Shutterstock; Marcel Jancovic/Shutterstock; mast3r/Shutterstock; Nick Barounis/Shutterstock; Pablo H Caridad/Shutterstock; sfam_photo/Shutterstock; Swapan/Shutterstock; Vince Clements/Shutterstock. pp18/19: CG Textures; Angela Jones/Shutterstock; Derek L Miller/Shutterstock; Ramona Heim/Shutterstock; Direct.gov.uk/Vector Portal; ktynzq/Shutterstock; Zacarias Pereira da Mata/Shutterstock; pp20/21: SarahAllenStock; Adolfo Rodriguez Aguilar/Shutterstock; ktynzq/Shutterstock; Milos Luzanin/Shutterstock; Picsfive/Shutterstock; VladKol/Shutterstock. pp22/23: CG Textures; Dgrilla/Shutterstock; HENX/Shutterstock; KSPhotography/Shutterstock; Olemac/Shutterstock; Dennis Steen/Shutterstock; Chad Gordon Higgins/Shutterstock; Sergey Kamshylin/Shutterstock; Terence Mendoza/Shutterstock; William Attard McCarthy/Shutterstock; Alex Long/York Museums Trust. pp24/25: Jcyoung/Dreamstime; 3drenderings/Shutterstock; Alfonso de Tomas/Shutterstock; Anneka/Shutterstock; Cindi L/Shutterstock; italianest/Shutterstock; Liz Van Steenburgh/Shutterstock; gualtiero boffi/Shutterstock; Markus Gann/Shutterstock; O.V.D./Shutterstock; Robert English/Shutterstock; Roman Sigaev/Shutterstock; Ronald Sumners/Shutterstock; Zacarias Pereira da Mata/Shutterstock; Zand/Shutterstock. pp26/27: CG Textures; ehoffbuhr; Freegraphicsource. com; Africa Studio/Shutterstock; Ecelop/Shutterstock; Laurent Renault/Shutterstock; pp28/29: CG Textures; David Arts/Shutterstock; Picsfive/Shutterstock. pp30/31: Angela Jones/Shutterstock; Borodaev/Shutterstock; Bragin Alexey/Shutterstock; F.C.G./Shutterstock; fotoret/Shutterstock; Pablo H Caridad/Shutterstock; Picsfive/Shutterstock; Robbi/Shutterstock; S.Dashkevych/Shutterstock; vladm/Shutterstock. p32: CG Textures.